How to Buy, Store, and Use Crypto Safely

Wallets, Exchanges, Scams to Avoid, and Secure Practices for First-Time Investors

By Joe Correa

Published by Live Stronger Faster

This book is for educational and informational purposes only. The author and publisher are not engaged in rendering legal, financial, or other professional advice. Readers should consult a qualified professional before making any financial decisions.

First Edition

Table of Contents

Introduction 5

Chapter 1: Choosing the Right Crypto Exchange 8

Chapter 2: Understanding Crypto Wallets: Hot vs. Cold Storage 16

Chapter 3: Avoiding Crypto Scams and Common Mistakes 24

Chapter 4: Making Your First Crypto Transaction Safely 31

Chapter 5: Using Crypto for Payments, Staking, and Passive Income 37

Chapter 6: Converting Crypto Back to Cash Safely 43

Chapter 7: Tracking Your Portfolio and Staying Organized 49

Chapter 8: Staying Safe with DeFi, NFTs, and Emerging Crypto Trends 55

Chapter 9: Building a Long-Term Crypto Strategy 61

Chapter 10: Keeping Up With Crypto and Adapting Your Plan 67

Epilogue: The Journey Ahead 73

Introduction

Cryptocurrency has completely transformed how we think about money, investment, and financial independence. But with great opportunity comes great responsibility. For every story of someone who doubled their savings in a bull run, there's someone who lost it all because they didn't understand how to store, protect, or even buy crypto properly.

That's where this book comes in. **"How to Buy, Store, and Use Crypto Safely"** is your real-world guide to getting started in crypto the right way. We won't just talk about theories — you'll get practical steps, tools, and examples that you can follow even if this is your very first exposure to digital currency.

We'll start by demystifying **how to buy cryptocurrency**. With hundreds of platforms, exchanges, and apps available, knowing which ones are legitimate, easy to use, and secure can save you time, money, and stress. We'll compare centralized exchanges like Coinbase and Binance with decentralized platforms, and help you identify what fits your level of experience and goals.

Next, we'll dive deep into one of the most misunderstood but essential parts of crypto: **wallets**. You'll learn the difference between **hot wallets** (like mobile apps or browser extensions) and **cold wallets** (hardware or offline options), and when to use each one. We'll walk you through how to set them up, secure them with best practices, and avoid costly mistakes like lost keys or phishing attacks.

Safety is a recurring theme throughout this book. As new investors pour into the crypto market, **scams are becoming more sophisticated** — from fake airdrops to malicious links and social media impersonators. We'll cover the **most common crypto scams**, how to spot them instantly, and how to protect yourself with simple habits, browser settings, and security layers that professionals use every day.

But this book isn't just about avoiding danger. It's about **empowering you to use your crypto in the real world** — from making your first transaction, to earning passive income through staking or using DeFi apps. You'll discover how to pay with crypto, send funds globally, and even plan your taxes and documentation ahead of time.

Whether you're just dipping your toes into Bitcoin, or ready to explore Ethereum, Solana, or other coins, this book will give you the confidence and tools to navigate the ecosystem securely.

By the end of this book, you'll know:

- How to choose the right exchange and wallet
- How to avoid the most common crypto scams
- The difference between custodial and non-custodial storage
- How to safely make your first crypto transaction
- Best practices for staying safe in an evolving digital landscape

This isn't just about buying crypto — it's about **protecting your future**. Let's get started.

Chapter 1: Choosing the Right Crypto Exchange

When you first step into the world of cryptocurrency, your very first real action is deciding where to buy it. This step might seem straightforward — pick a website or an app, create an account, and start buying. But in reality, choosing the right crypto exchange can be the difference between smooth sailing and a financial nightmare. Exchanges vary drastically in **security, fees, accessibility, and features**, and as a first-time investor, you'll want to make this choice with clarity and caution.

Let's start with the two main types of exchanges: **centralized exchanges (CEXs)** and **decentralized exchanges (DEXs)**. Centralized exchanges, such as Coinbase, Binance, Kraken, and Gemini, operate much like online banks or stock brokerages. They hold your funds in custodial wallets, manage order books, and offer customer service. For beginners, these are often the easiest starting point because they allow you to connect a bank account or credit card, buy crypto instantly, and trade with a user-friendly interface. However, there's a trade-off — since the exchange holds your crypto for you, you don't have full control over your private keys. This means if the platform is hacked or freezes withdrawals, your assets could be at risk.

On the other hand, **decentralized exchanges** like Uniswap, PancakeSwap, and SushiSwap allow peer-to-peer trading without a central authority. You connect your own wallet (usually a hot wallet like MetaMask), and you remain in control of your funds at all times. This reduces the risk of a centralized hack, but it comes with a steeper learning curve and no customer service to help you if you make a mistake. For complete beginners, DEXs can be intimidating — but they're worth learning about as your knowledge grows, because they offer freedom, privacy, and access to tokens that aren't listed on major CEXs.

Security should be your number one deciding factor when choosing an exchange. Look for platforms that offer **two-factor authentication (2FA)**, withdrawal address whitelisting, cold storage for the majority of customer funds, and a history of strong security practices. Avoid platforms that are too new, have unclear ownership, or lack transparency about how they store user funds. A quick search for "exchange name + hack" can reveal a lot about its track record.

Regulation and location also matter. Exchanges operating in the U.S., for example, must comply with strict KYC (Know

Your Customer) and AML (Anti-Money Laundering) regulations. This means you'll need to verify your identity with a government-issued ID before you can deposit or withdraw significant amounts. While this may feel invasive, regulated exchanges offer more legal protection in case something goes wrong. On the other hand, some international exchanges may offer looser restrictions, but you'll be trading off certain protections.

Next, compare **fees**. Exchanges make money by charging trading fees, withdrawal fees, and sometimes even deposit fees. For small, frequent trades, low trading fees are essential. Some platforms offer **maker/taker models** where providing liquidity (maker orders) costs less than taking liquidity (market orders). Others offer fee discounts for holding their native token — for example, Binance offers lower fees if you pay them using BNB.

Ease of use is another crucial factor, especially for first-time buyers. Look for an exchange with a clean, intuitive interface and a responsive mobile app. Some platforms cater to advanced traders with detailed charts and order types like limit, stop-limit, and trailing stop orders. While these are useful tools, a cluttered interface can overwhelm beginners, so you might prefer a simple "buy/sell" interface at first.

Liquidity is often overlooked by new investors, but it plays a huge role in your ability to trade without major slippage. High-liquidity exchanges can handle large trades without significantly affecting the market price, whereas low-liquidity platforms can cause you to pay more than you expect. Checking an exchange's daily trading volume can help you gauge its liquidity.

Finally, consider **customer support and reputation**. Before committing, try contacting the platform's support team with a simple question and see how quickly they respond. A responsive team is invaluable when dealing with potential deposit or withdrawal issues. Reading user reviews, checking community forums like Reddit, and seeing how the exchange handles complaints can reveal its commitment to customer satisfaction.

In summary, the perfect exchange for a beginner will likely be a well-known, regulated, and secure centralized platform with strong customer support and reasonable fees. As you gain confidence, you can branch out to decentralized exchanges for more control and opportunities. Remember: your exchange is your first gateway into the crypto world — choose wisely, and it will serve as a reliable foundation for your investing journey.

How Ethan began his crypto story

Ethan had always been curious about cryptocurrency, but for years it felt like something other people did — the kind of people who lived on tech forums, built their own computers, and spoke in a language full of acronyms. But when his younger cousin mentioned doubling her money in just three months by investing in Ethereum, Ethan decided it was time to stop watching from the sidelines.

On a quiet Saturday morning, coffee in hand, he opened his laptop and typed, "How to buy Bitcoin" into the search bar. Hundreds of results popped up, each claiming to be the easiest, safest, or fastest way to start. Within minutes, Ethan was staring at a list of exchanges: Coinbase, Binance, Kraken, Gemini, Crypto.com, and a dozen others he'd never heard of. The choices were overwhelming.

He clicked on the first option — a sleek website promising "instant Bitcoin purchases with zero fees." But something about it felt off. The site had no physical address listed, no real company information, and the reviews online were mixed. "Scam," one Reddit post read. "Lost everything." Ethan quickly closed the tab, a knot forming in his stomach. This was his first lesson: just because a platform looks professional doesn't mean it's trustworthy.

Determined to do it right, he started digging deeper. He learned there were two main types of exchanges: **centralized** and **decentralized**. Centralized exchanges were like banks — they held your money for you and offered a friendly interface, perfect for beginners. Decentralized exchanges let you trade directly from your own wallet without handing your coins over to anyone. That sounded safer, but the step-by-step guides he found for using them looked more like programming tutorials than something an everyday investor could follow. For now, he decided to stick with centralized exchanges until he understood the basics.

Ethan narrowed his list to three: Coinbase for its ease of use, Kraken for its reputation, and Binance for its low fees and wide selection of coins. He compared their security features, learning about two-factor authentication, withdrawal whitelists, and cold storage. He even searched "Coinbase hack" and "Binance hack" just to see how each platform handled past incidents. Coinbase had strong insurance coverage for U.S. customers. Binance, while global and more flexible, had been hacked in 2019 — but quickly reimbursed all affected users. That gave him confidence in their customer protection policies.

Next came the topic of fees. Ethan had no plans to invest thousands right away, so the trading fees needed to be fair.

Coinbase's fees were higher but the interface was incredibly beginner-friendly. Binance's fees were lower, and Kraken's were somewhere in the middle. He read about "maker" and "taker" fees but decided that for now, the small difference didn't matter — what mattered was avoiding hidden charges and withdrawal costs.

As he explored further, Ethan discovered the importance of **liquidity**. He had no idea that low trading volume on an exchange could make him pay more for the same amount of crypto. It was like trying to buy an obscure brand of coffee in a small store — the price could spike just because there wasn't enough stock. Large exchanges like Binance and Coinbase had massive daily trading volumes, which meant better prices and faster order fulfillment.

Still, one question nagged at him: What if something went wrong and he needed help? He decided to test the customer service. He sent a simple question to each exchange about their withdrawal limits. Coinbase replied within two hours, Kraken in six, and Binance the next day. It was clear who took customer support seriously.

By the end of the weekend, Ethan had made his choice. He signed up for Coinbase to make his first purchase, knowing he could branch out to Binance later for more advanced trading.

The onboarding was smooth: he uploaded his ID, linked his bank account, and was ready to buy within minutes. He set up two-factor authentication, wrote down his backup codes on paper (not online), and triple-checked that his account recovery settings were in place.

A week later, Ethan made his first purchase — $200 worth of Bitcoin. It wasn't much, but it was a start. He knew the real value wasn't just in the coins he bought, but in the process he'd gone through to choose where to buy them. Instead of jumping in blindly, he had taken the time to understand the risks, compare his options, and make an informed decision.

That night, as he checked his small but growing portfolio, Ethan smiled. He wasn't just an observer anymore — he was officially part of the crypto world. And thanks to the research he'd done, he felt confident he had taken his first step the right way.

Chapter 2: Understanding Crypto Wallets: Hot vs. Cold Storage

Buying cryptocurrency is just the first step. The real challenge — and the part that separates beginners who succeed from those who lose their investment — is **storing it safely**. In the crypto world, there's an old saying: *"Not your keys, not your coins."* This simple phrase means that if you don't control the private keys to your wallet, you don't truly control your crypto. And understanding how wallets work is the key to keeping your funds secure.

A **crypto wallet** is not like a physical wallet that holds cash or cards. Instead, it's a digital tool that stores the cryptographic keys — your **public key** (like your account number) and your **private key** (like your password) — that give you access to your cryptocurrency. The coins themselves are stored on the blockchain, but without your keys, you can't access them.

Wallets generally fall into two main categories: **hot wallets** and **cold wallets**.

Hot wallets are connected to the internet. They include mobile apps like Trust Wallet, desktop programs like Exodus, and browser extensions like MetaMask. They are convenient because you can access your crypto quickly to send, receive, or trade. However, this convenience comes with a risk: anything connected to the internet is a potential target for hackers, malware, or phishing attacks. For small amounts or frequent transactions, hot wallets are practical — but they are not ideal for long-term storage of large holdings.

Cold wallets, on the other hand, are completely offline. They include hardware wallets like Ledger Nano X and Trezor, as well as paper wallets that store your keys physically. Since they are not connected to the internet, cold wallets are far less vulnerable to hacking. The trade-off is that they require more steps to access and use. For serious investors who plan to hold significant amounts of crypto for months or years, cold wallets are the gold standard for security.

When choosing between hot and cold wallets, think of it like a checking account versus a safe deposit box. Your checking account (hot wallet) is where you keep spending money for daily use — convenient but more exposed. Your safe deposit box (cold wallet) is where you store valuables you don't need every day — less convenient, but much safer.

Another important consideration is **custodial vs. non-custodial wallets**. A **custodial wallet** is controlled by a third party, such as the exchange where you purchased your crypto. They manage your private keys, which means you don't have to worry about losing them — but it also means you're trusting them with your assets. A **non-custodial wallet** puts you in full control of your keys and funds. While this gives you complete ownership, it also means you are solely responsible for security. If you lose your private keys or recovery phrase no one can help you retrieve your crypto.

Speaking of recovery phrases, also known as **seed phrases** this is perhaps the single most important security feature of your wallet. A seed phrase is a list of 12 to 24 random words generated when you create a wallet. It's your master key — anyone who has it can access your funds. This phrase should never be stored on a device connected to the internet, and certainly never shared with anyone. The safest practice is to write it down on paper, store multiple copies in secure locations, or even engrave it on a metal plate for fire and water resistance.

Another layer of protection is **multi-signature wallets** (multi-sig). These require multiple private keys to authorize a transaction. This can be useful for business accounts or joint holdings, where more than one person must approve before funds can move. While not essential for beginners understanding that this option exists can help you as your crypto portfolio grows.

It's also wise to consider **backup and redundancy**. Hardware wallets can break, mobile wallets can be lost if your phone is damaged, and paper wallets can deteriorate. Having secure backups ensures that no single accident can wipe out your holdings.

Finally, understand that security is not a one-time action — it's a habit. Regularly update your wallet software or firmware to patch vulnerabilities. Enable two-factor authentication where possible. Be cautious of fake wallet apps in app stores or phishing sites designed to mimic legitimate wallet providers.

The bottom line is this: **Your wallet is your vault**. Just as you wouldn't leave piles of cash in your car's glove compartment, you shouldn't leave significant amounts of crypto on an exchange or in an unsecured hot wallet. By learning how wallets work, choosing the right type for your needs, and following strong security practices, you ensure that your investment remains safe no matter what happens in the market.

How Ethan discovered hot wallet

A month after buying his first Bitcoin, Ethan's confidence had grown. His Coinbase account showed a small but satisfying profit, and he had started telling friends about his investment.

One evening over dinner, his coworker, Lucas, leaned across the table and asked, “So... where are you keeping it?”

Ethan laughed. “On Coinbase, of course. Where else?”

Lucas’s expression shifted to concern. “That’s fine for now, but you know the saying, right? Not your keys, not your coins.”

Ethan had heard the phrase online but never paid it much attention. Lucas explained that when his Bitcoin sat on Coinbase, the exchange actually controlled the private keys. If something happened — a hack, an account freeze, or even a government order — Ethan might not be able to access his own funds.

That night, Ethan couldn’t shake the thought. He began researching “crypto wallets” and found himself pulled into a whole new world. He learned that a wallet wasn’t a leather pouch on your phone or a digital image on a screen — it was the tool that stored his cryptographic keys. Without those keys, the Bitcoin he thought he owned wasn’t really his.

The first type he discovered was the **hot wallet**. These were apps and software connected to the internet, like MetaMask or Trust Wallet. They were fast, easy to set up, and perfect for quick transactions. Ethan downloaded Trust Wallet just to see how it worked. In minutes, he had a sleek, colorful app on his phone showing empty balances for dozens of coins. But then came the seed phrase — twelve random words he was told to write down and store somewhere safe. A warning flashed: *"Never share this with anyone."*

He wrote the words on a scrap of paper and stuffed it in his desk drawer. Then, remembering Lucas's advice, he felt uneasy. What if the paper got lost or his apartment caught fire? What if someone broke in and found it? Suddenly, that quick setup didn't feel as secure as he thought.

Digging deeper, Ethan learned about **cold wallets**. The idea fascinated him: a device, like a USB stick, that kept his keys completely offline. Hackers couldn't touch it because it wasn't connected to the internet. He read glowing reviews about Ledger Nano X and Trezor, but balked at spending $80–$150 for a piece of hardware. Still, the stories of people losing their life savings in exchange hacks convinced him it was worth the investment.

Two days later, a small package arrived at his door — his brand-new Ledger. The unboxing felt like opening a high-tech safe. Inside was a sleek black device, a USB cable, and a card for writing down the recovery phrase. The setup took him through each step carefully, even forcing him to physically press both buttons on the device to approve actions. It was slow, deliberate, and oddly reassuring.

When it came time to transfer his Bitcoin from Coinbase to the Ledger, Ethan hesitated. What if he messed it up and the coins vanished into the digital void? He double-checked the receiving address, confirmed it character by character, and finally hit “send.” A few minutes later, the Ledger screen lit up with the balance. His Bitcoin was officially in his possession.

Feeling proud, Ethan told Lucas the next day. Lucas nodded. “Now you’re playing in the big leagues. You control your keys, you control your coins.”

Ethan realized that wallets weren’t just about storage — they were about **ownership and security**. His hot wallet was like carrying a small amount of cash in his pocket for quick spending. His cold wallet was the vault where his real savings lived.

From then on, Ethan developed a ritual. Every time he made a new crypto purchase, he would keep a small portion in his hot wallet for easy access, and move the rest to his cold wallet. He made multiple copies of his recovery phrase, storing them in separate, secure locations. He even engraved one on a small stainless steel plate after reading about fireproof backups.

The more he learned, the more Ethan understood that this extra effort wasn't paranoia — it was preparation. Markets could crash, exchanges could disappear overnight, but as long as he had his keys and his backups, his crypto was safe.

For the first time since starting his crypto journey, Ethan didn't just feel like an investor. He felt like a custodian of his own digital wealth.

Chapter 3: Avoiding Crypto Scams and Common Mistakes

The cryptocurrency market is full of opportunity — but it's also full of traps. Because crypto transactions are irreversible and decentralized, there's no "fraud department" to reverse a bad transaction. Once your coins are gone, they're gone for good. This reality makes crypto a prime target for scammers, who are constantly inventing new schemes to separate investors from their money. Understanding the most common scams and mistakes is essential if you want to protect your assets and grow your portfolio safely.

One of the most widespread scams in crypto is **phishing**. Just like in traditional finance, phishing happens when a fraudster tricks you into revealing sensitive information, such as your wallet's private key or seed phrase. In crypto, this often comes in the form of fake emails or websites designed to look like legitimate exchanges or wallet providers. They might send you an urgent warning claiming your account has been compromised, urging you to "log in" through their link — which actually leads to a fraudulent site. Always check the URL carefully, avoid clicking suspicious links, and go directly to the official website when in doubt.

Another dangerous scam is the **fake wallet or app**. Cybercriminals create counterfeit versions of popular wallet apps and upload them to app stores, complete with convincing logos and fake reviews. When unsuspecting users download them, their private keys are stolen the moment they import their seed phrase. To avoid this, only download wallet apps from official websites or verified app store links, and double-check the publisher's name before installing.

Social media is also a hotbed for scams. **Impersonation scams** involve fraudsters posing as well-known figures in crypto — influencers, exchange CEOs, or even your friends — and offering "giveaways" where you send them coins to "receive double in return." These are always fake. No legitimate entity will ever ask you to send them money to get more back. Similarly, **pump-and-dump schemes** are common in online crypto groups. Scammers hype up a little-known coin, convincing investors to buy in, then sell their holdings at the peak, causing the price to crash.

Then there are **airdrop scams**. While real airdrops do exist (where projects distribute free tokens to promote their platform), scammers exploit this concept by sending malicious tokens to your wallet. When you attempt to interact with these tokens — even just viewing their contract details — it can give them access to your funds. The safest approach is to ignore unsolicited tokens entirely.

Aside from scams, many beginners lose money through **common mistakes**. One of the biggest is sending coins to the wrong wallet address. Crypto transactions are final — if you mistype even one character, your funds could be lost forever. Always copy and paste addresses, then double-check the first and last few characters before sending.

Another frequent mistake is **keeping all funds on an exchange**. Exchanges can be hacked or shut down, and users who store their crypto there risk losing access to their assets. The best practice is to transfer long-term holdings to a secure non-custodial wallet, preferably a cold wallet.

Neglecting security practices is also a costly error. Using weak passwords, skipping two-factor authentication, or storing your seed phrase on a cloud service makes it easier for attackers to compromise your accounts. Security in crypto is a constant process — you must remain proactive.

Finally, beginners often fall victim to **FOMO (Fear of Missing Out)**, buying into coins because they're trending without doing proper research. Many of these coins are short-lived hype projects that collapse within weeks. The safest approach is to research thoroughly before investing and to never risk money you can't afford to lose.

In the crypto world, skepticism is your ally. Always verify, never rush, and remember: if something sounds too good to be true, it almost always is. By recognizing common scams and avoiding beginner mistakes, you can keep your investment safe and position yourself for long-term success.

When Ethan's account was locked

It had been three months since Ethan first stepped into the world of crypto, and his confidence was growing. His Bitcoin sat safely in his Ledger, and he had even added a small amount of Ethereum to his portfolio. But one Thursday morning, an email caught his attention. The subject line read: **"Urgent Security Notice: Your Coinbase Account is Locked"**.

The email looked official — it had the Coinbase logo, professional formatting, and even a warning in red text urging him to click a link to "verify his account." Ethan's pulse quickened. The idea of losing access to his funds was unsettling. But just as he was about to click, he remembered a YouTube video he'd watched about **phishing scams**. He hovered over the link and saw the URL: *coinbsae-secure-login.com*. One extra letter. That tiny detail was all it took to confirm it was a fake. He deleted the email immediately, feeling both relieved and a little shaken.

A week later, while scrolling through the app store, Ethan decided to try a new wallet app he'd heard about in a Telegram group. He found one with the right name, good ratings, and an appealing design. Just before downloading, he hesitated. He'd read that scammers sometimes upload **fake wallet apps** designed to steal your private keys. He went to the official website of the wallet provider, clicked the app store link from there, and realized the version he had almost downloaded was an imposter. The logo was slightly off, and the developer name didn't match. It was another close call.

His third brush with danger came from social media. One evening, Ethan saw a Twitter post from a verified account — or so it appeared — claiming to be from a well-known crypto influencer. The post announced a special "giveaway" where anyone who sent 0.1 ETH to a certain address would receive 0.2 ETH back. The comments were full of people claiming they had already doubled their money. For a moment, the temptation was real. But then he spotted the subtle misspelling in the influencer's handle and realized it was an **impersonation scam**. He reported the account and moved on.

Not all dangers came from outright scams — some were the result of **simple mistakes**. Ethan remembered the first time he almost sent crypto to the wrong address. A friend had given him a wallet address over text, and he began typing it manually into his Ledger Live app. Halfway through, he realized that even one wrong character would send the funds into a digital void forever. From that day forward, he swore to always copy and paste addresses and verify the first and last four characters before hitting "send."

He also made a new rule: never keep more than a small amount of crypto on an exchange. While it was convenient to leave his coins there for quick trades, he knew exchanges could be hacked or shut down without warning. Moving his holdings into his cold wallet after every major purchase became part of his routine.

Perhaps the most valuable lesson came from a moment of pure **FOMO**. A friend messaged him about a small altcoin that was "going to the moon" and doubling in price every hour. Ethan nearly bought in on impulse, but stopped to do his own research. The project's website was vague, the team was anonymous, and the tokenomics didn't make sense. Two days later, the coin's price collapsed by 90%. That close call taught him that hype without substance was just another form of risk.

By the end of the year, Ethan's portfolio wasn't massive, but it was intact — and that, he realized, was worth more than any short-term gains. He had learned that the crypto market rewards caution as much as courage. Scams and mistakes would always be part of the landscape, but as long as he stayed vigilant, skeptical, and disciplined, he could navigate the digital frontier with confidence.

Chapter 4: Making Your First Crypto Transaction Safely

Sending or receiving cryptocurrency for the first time is a milestone — it's when your crypto stops being just a number in your account and becomes something you actively use. But because blockchain transactions are permanent, there's no "undo" button. One wrong move can result in lost funds that can never be recovered. That's why taking a careful, methodical approach is essential.

The first step is understanding the **transaction process**. Every crypto transfer involves a **sending address**, a **receiving address**, and the **amount** of cryptocurrency being sent. The sending address is controlled by your wallet, and the receiving address is provided by the person or platform you want to send funds to. Each cryptocurrency has its own address format — Bitcoin addresses look different from Ethereum addresses, and sending the wrong coin to the wrong type of address will almost always result in permanent loss.

Before making a transaction, double-check you're using the correct **blockchain network**. For example, USDT (Tether) exists on multiple blockchains — Ethereum (ERC-20), Binance Smart Chain (BEP-20), and Tron (TRC-20) among others. Sending USDT from one network to an address on another network will result in failed or lost funds. Most wallets will warn you if the networks don't match, but it's your responsibility to confirm before sending.

When sending, **copy and paste** the recipient's wallet address — never type it manually. Even one wrong character will send your coins to the wrong place. After pasting, always verify the first four and last four characters of the address. If your wallet supports it, enable **address whitelisting**, which locks withdrawals to pre-approved addresses only.

For your first transaction, it's wise to send a **small test amount** before transferring larger sums. This lets you confirm that the address and network are correct without risking a significant loss. Once the test amount arrives successfully, you can send the full amount.

Every transaction on the blockchain incurs a **network fee** (sometimes called a gas fee). Fees vary depending on the blockchain and how busy it is at the time. On networks like Ethereum, gas fees can spike during high demand, so you may want to check current fees using tools like *Etherscan Gas Tracker* or *Blockchain.com Fee Charts* before sending.

Once you've entered the details and confirmed the transaction in your wallet, the network will process it. Depending on the blockchain, it may take anywhere from a few seconds to an hour for full confirmation. Bitcoin transactions, for example, are usually considered secure after six confirmations, which might take 30–60 minutes.

When receiving crypto, the process is simpler — you provide your public address to the sender, and the funds are sent directly to your wallet. But you still need to be cautious. Make sure you're giving the correct address for the correct coin and network. If you accidentally provide your Ethereum address for a Bitcoin transaction, the coins will be lost.

If you're making a payment to a business or exchange, be aware that they may use **unique deposit addresses** for each customer or transaction. Always copy the deposit address from your account dashboard, and avoid reusing old addresses unless the platform explicitly allows it.

For added safety, consider using a **QR code** to share addresses when possible. This reduces the risk of typos or copy-paste errors and is especially useful for in-person transactions. Just be sure the QR code is generated by your wallet or trusted platform, not a third-party app.

Finally, always check your wallet or blockchain explorer after sending or receiving funds. Blockchain explorers (like *Etherscan*, *Blockchain.com*, or *Solscan*) allow you to verify that your transaction has been recorded on the blockchain and to see its current status.

Your first crypto transaction should never be rushed. By confirming addresses, networks, and amounts, using test transactions, and understanding fees, you can build the habits that will keep your transfers smooth and safe for years to come.

Now, lets about how Ethan built his crypto holdings

Ethan had been building up his crypto holdings for months, but he had yet to actually send any to someone else. Everything he'd purchased was sitting in his Ledger or a small amount in his Trust Wallet. Then one afternoon, his friend Olivia asked if she could pay him back for concert tickets in Ethereum instead of cash. "It's easier," she said. "And you'll get to make your first real crypto transaction."

Excited, Ethan agreed. He opened his Trust Wallet and tapped "Receive." A long string of letters and numbers appeared – his Ethereum address. He copied it and sent it to Olivia. She replied almost instantly: "Got it. Sending now."

Before long, Ethan saw a pending transaction in his wallet. It was thrilling to watch the little spinning icon, knowing money was moving through the blockchain straight to him. Ten minutes later, the ETH appeared in his balance. But Olivia had sent more than they agreed on by mistake. She messaged, "Oops, can you send back 0.05 ETH?"

This was the moment Ethan had been waiting for — his first outgoing transaction. He opened the "Send" screen and pasted Olivia's address from her message. Then, remembering something he'd read, he double-checked the first and last four characters of the address. His stomach dropped — they didn't match the address she had used earlier. Somewhere between copying and pasting, a malicious program could have swapped the address — a known **clipboard hijacking** trick.

Ethan called Olivia right away. She sent her correct address again, but this time he scanned it as a QR code instead of copying it. He entered the amount, then paused. "Better safe than sorry," he thought, and sent a tiny test amount first. A few minutes later, Olivia confirmed she received it. Only then did Ethan send the full 0.05 ETH.

The transaction cost a small gas fee, and he noticed how much it fluctuated depending on the time of day. He made a mental note to check gas prices before future transactions. Later, curious about the process, he opened Etherscan and searched for his wallet address. There it was — a complete public record of both his incoming and outgoing transactions, each with its own unique hash. Seeing the transparency of the blockchain in action gave him a new appreciation for how the system worked.

A few weeks later, Ethan tried paying for something online using Bitcoin — a hardware wallet accessory. The site gave him a Bitcoin address and a QR code. He sent a test payment again this time using his Ledger. It felt slow compared to Ethereum taking nearly 30 minutes for the merchant to confirm. But it worked, and he knew that no bank or payment processor had been involved.

That night, Ethan reflected on the experience. He realized how easy it would have been to make a mistake: sending to the wrong network, entering the wrong address, skipping the test transaction. These were irreversible errors that could have cost him hundreds of dollars. But by moving deliberately, verifying every detail, and using small test amounts, he had turned what could have been a stressful event into a confident step forward

For Ethan, making his first crypto transactions wasn't just about sending coins — it was about proving to himself that he could navigate the process without falling into common traps It was one more layer of confidence in his growing journey through the digital economy.

Chapter 5: Using Crypto for Payments, Staking, and Passive Income

For many people, buying and holding cryptocurrency is just the beginning. The real power of crypto lies in how you can use it — not only as a payment method, but also as a tool to generate passive income. Whether you're buying goods and services, staking your coins to earn rewards, or participating in lending platforms, there are safe and smart ways to put your assets to work.

The simplest and most immediate use of crypto is **making payments**. Today, thousands of businesses worldwide accept Bitcoin, Ethereum, and other major cryptocurrencies as payment. Some accept them directly, while others use payment processors like BitPay or Coinbase Commerce to handle the conversion into local currency. Paying with crypto is often faster and cheaper for international transactions compared to traditional bank wires, and it avoids currency conversion fees. However, you must be careful to send the correct amount, use the right blockchain network, and ensure the recipient is reputable before making any transaction. Because crypto prices are volatile, it's common for merchants to require payment within a short time window, so always confirm the details quickly.

Beyond spending, one of the most popular ways to use crypto is **staking**. Staking involves locking up a certain amount of cryptocurrency to support the operations of a blockchain network — most commonly, those using proof-of-stake (PoS) consensus mechanisms like Ethereum, Cardano, and Solana. In return for staking your coins, you receive rewards, usually in the form of additional tokens. The annual percentage yield (APY) varies depending on the network, but staking can be an attractive way to earn a steady return on assets you were planning to hold anyway. However, staking often requires you to lock your coins for a set period, and if the coin's price drops, the value of your rewards could be offset by the loss in market value.

Another avenue for passive income is **crypto lending**. This involves lending your coins to other users via centralized lending platforms like BlockFi or Nexo, or through decentralized finance (DeFi) protocols like Aave and Compound. In exchange, you earn interest, often higher than what traditional banks offer. The main risk here is counterparty risk — if the platform or protocol fails, you could lose your funds. That's why it's important to choose reputable platforms, diversify across multiple services, and avoid putting all your holdings into a single lending program.

For more advanced users, **yield farming** and **liquidity**

provision are ways to earn additional rewards by supplying crypto to decentralized exchanges. In liquidity pools, you deposit pairs of cryptocurrencies into a smart contract, enabling others to trade them. You earn a portion of the trading fees plus potential bonus tokens. While the returns can be high, these strategies carry risks like impermanent loss — a situation where the value of your staked tokens changes compared to simply holding them.

If you prefer low-risk passive income, you can explore **stablecoin staking or lending**. Because stablecoins are pegged to a fiat currency like the US dollar, they are less volatile, making them ideal for earning interest without as much price fluctuation risk. Many platforms offer attractive APYs for stablecoin deposits, though you should still vet the platform's security and reputation.

A crucial consideration in all these activities is **tax implications**. In many countries, using crypto for payments triggers a taxable event if the asset has appreciated since you acquired it. Likewise, staking rewards and interest from lending are often treated as income. Keep accurate records of every transaction, reward, and payout to simplify tax reporting.

Finally, never forget the **security layer**. Using your crypto for payments or passive income means interacting with third parties, smart contracts, or networks outside your personal wallet. Always verify addresses, read terms carefully, research the platform's history, and consider starting with small amounts to test the process before committing significant funds.

Using crypto actively — whether for spending or earning — can expand your financial freedom and open up new opportunities. But just like buying and storing it, the key to success is a balance of cautious research, sound judgment, and secure habits.

Ethan's story on how he learned about staking

Ethan's first few months in crypto had been all about buying, storing, and protecting his coins. But one Saturday morning, while browsing online for a new laptop bag, he noticed something different in the checkout options — alongside Visa, Mastercard, and PayPal, there was a small orange Bitcoin logo. Underneath it read: *"Pay with Bitcoin or Ethereum."*

The idea excited him. Paying with crypto felt like the ultimate test of being part of the digital economy. He selected the Bitcoin option, copied the payment address, and pasted it into his Ledger Live app. Before confirming, he remembered his rule: always check the first and last few characters of the address. They matched perfectly. Still cautious, he sent a small test payment first. Ten minutes later, the merchant's site updated with a green checkmark: *Payment received.* Confident, he sent the full amount. The whole process took less than half an hour — no banks, no card processors, no currency conversion fees. It felt almost futuristic.

That first purchase opened Ethan's mind to other possibilities. A few weeks later, while talking to Lucas, he learned about **staking**. "You're just letting your coins sit there," Lucas said. "Why not make them work for you?" Lucas explained how staking Ethereum could earn passive rewards over time. Intrigued, Ethan researched staking platforms and decided to start small with Cardano (ADA). He delegated a portion of his ADA to a reputable staking pool directly from his wallet. The interface told him his coins would remain in his control, and rewards would be paid out every five days. A week later, he saw his first tiny staking reward — just a fraction of an ADA coin, but it felt like a glimpse into the future of earning.

Encouraged, Ethan explored other ways to grow his holdings. He came across a reputable centralized lending platform that allowed him to deposit stablecoins and earn interest. The rates were higher than his bank savings account, and the idea of earning passive income without worrying about price swings was appealing. He transferred a small amount of USDC and watched as interest began accumulating daily. Still, he remained cautious — he read the platform's terms twice, researched its insurance policies, and decided not to deposit more than he could afford to lose.

Not all experiments were perfect. Ethan tried providing liquidity on a decentralized exchange after reading about **yield farming** in a forum. The rewards looked great on paper, but he quickly learned about "impermanent loss" when the value of one of the coins in his pair dropped significantly. While he didn't lose everything, the experience taught him that high returns often came with high risks.

Over the months, Ethan built a balanced approach. He kept the majority of his crypto in secure cold storage, allocated a portion for staking, used stablecoins for low-risk lending, and kept a small amount in hot wallets for payments. Every time he received a staking reward or saw interest credited to his account, it reinforced his belief that crypto wasn't just about speculation — it was a tool for creating ongoing income streams.

One evening, while checking his staking rewards and lending interest, Ethan realized something important: his portfolio was no longer just a static investment. It was a living system, working quietly in the background, earning him money while he slept. For someone who had once been afraid to make his first purchase, the shift felt both empowering and liberating.

Chapter 6: Converting Crypto Back to Cash Safely

At some point in your crypto journey, you may decide to convert part of your holdings back into traditional currency. This could be to lock in profits, pay for an expense, or simply diversify your assets. While buying crypto is often straightforward, cashing out requires just as much — if not more — attention to detail. Done carelessly, you could face unnecessary fees, tax headaches, or even security risks.

The first step is choosing **where** to sell your crypto. The most common option is a **centralized exchange (CEX)** like Coinbase, Kraken, or Binance. These platforms allow you to trade your cryptocurrency for fiat currency (such as USD, EUR, or GBP) and then withdraw it to your linked bank account. When using a CEX, make sure your account is fully verified to avoid withdrawal delays or limits. For beginners, this is usually the simplest and most secure method, as regulated exchanges follow established banking procedures.

Another option is **peer-to-peer (P2P) marketplaces**, such as Binance P2P, LocalBitcoins, or Paxful. Here, you sell directly to another person using agreed-upon payment methods like bank transfers, PayPal, or cash in person. While P2P trading can offer better rates, it carries higher risk, so always use platforms with strong escrow systems that hold the buyer's funds until you confirm receipt of payment. If meeting in person, choose public, secure locations and avoid carrying large amounts of cash alone.

A third method is using **crypto debit cards** provided by companies like Crypto.com, Binance, or BitPay. These cards let you spend your crypto directly anywhere debit cards are accepted, automatically converting it to fiat at the point of sale. While convenient, keep in mind that each transaction may be a taxable event, and conversion fees may apply.

Before you sell, always check the **conversion rate and fees**. Exchange rates can vary between platforms, and withdrawal fees differ depending on the method you choose. If selling a large amount, you might want to monitor the market for a few days to secure a favorable price, but be mindful that crypto is volatile and prices can change quickly.

Once you've chosen your method, the process generally involves transferring your crypto from your wallet to the selling platform. This is where extra caution is essential — make sure you're sending the correct coin to the correct address. Sending Bitcoin to an Ethereum address or vice versa will result in irreversible loss. Always triple-check wallet addresses, and if you're moving a large sum, send a small test transaction first.

Tax reporting is one of the most overlooked parts of converting crypto to cash. In many countries, selling crypto at a profit triggers capital gains tax, and even exchanging one cryptocurrency for another can be taxable. Keep detailed records of when you bought your crypto, how much you paid, and when and for how much you sold it. Many exchanges offer downloadable transaction histories, but you should also consider using crypto tax software like CoinTracker, Koinly, or TokenTax to stay organized and compliant.

Security is critical when cashing out. Scammers often target people trying to sell crypto, offering "better rates" or convincing you to bypass official platforms. Stick to reputable services, enable two-factor authentication, and avoid sharing screenshots or details of your transactions on public forums. If you're using a bank account for withdrawals, make sure it's in your name to prevent delays or holds.

Finally, have a **cash-out strategy**. Decide in advance how much you want to convert, why you're converting it, and whether it makes sense to sell all at once or in stages. Some investors choose to sell gradually to reduce the impact of short-term price swings.

Converting crypto to cash is not just about getting your money — it's about doing so in a way that is safe, tax-efficient, and aligned with your financial goals. By selecting the right platform, verifying every step, and keeping good records, you can move smoothly from digital assets back to traditional currency without unnecessary stress or risk.

How Ethan transferred Bitcoin back to cash

Ethan had been holding onto his crypto for almost a year, watching the value rise and fall with each market swing. Lately, Bitcoin had been climbing steadily, and he decided it was time to take some profit. Not all of it — just enough to cover a few expenses and reward himself for staying disciplined.

His first thought was to simply hit the "Sell" button in his Coinbase app, but Lucas's voice echoed in his head: "Don't rush. Cashing out is just as important as buying in." Ethan decided to plan his withdrawal carefully. He began by checking which platforms he could use. Coinbase was the obvious choice, but he also looked into Kraken and Binance to compare fees and conversion rates. To his surprise, the difference between platforms could mean an extra $50–$100 on the amount he planned to withdraw.

He chose Coinbase for its ease of use and direct connection to his bank account. After logging in, he noticed a banner reminding him to ensure his identity verification was up to date. If it wasn't, large withdrawals could be delayed. Thankfully, his account was already verified from when he started.

Ethan transferred the Bitcoin he wanted to sell from his Ledger to Coinbase. This made him nervous — it was the largest transaction he'd ever sent. He copied the deposit address, verified the first and last four characters, and then sent a small test amount. Once it cleared, he moved the full amount. Within minutes, his Coinbase balance updated, showing the funds ready to sell.

He sold his Bitcoin for U.S. dollars and initiated a withdrawal to his bank account. The process was smooth, but the exchange estimated it would take 1–3 business days for the funds to arrive. Ethan had heard of **peer-to-peer selling** being faster, where you could get money the same day, but he preferred the safety of a regulated platform over meeting strangers or risking a disputed payment.

While waiting for the transfer, he started reading about taxes on crypto sales. He realized that selling at a profit meant he'd owe capital gains tax, and the exact amount depended on how long he'd held the Bitcoin and the difference between his purchase price and selling price. Fortunately, he had kept meticulous records, including screenshots and CSV downloads from both Coinbase and his Ledger transactions. This made calculating his gains much easier.

Two days later, Ethan saw the deposit in his bank account. It felt satisfying to have converted part of his digital assets into real-world cash, but he also felt a sense of responsibility. He moved a portion into savings, set some aside for taxes, and used a small amount to treat himself to a weekend getaway.

The experience taught him that cashing out wasn't something to do on impulse. It required planning, careful execution, and awareness of both fees and taxes. From that day on, he made a rule for himself: whenever he took profits, he would do it in stages, not all at once, to reduce risk and avoid bad timing.

Ethan now understood that selling crypto wasn't the "end" of his investment journey — it was simply another step in managing it wisely. And just like buying, storing, and using it, the key to success was staying informed and making decisions with both caution and confidence.

Chapter 7: Tracking Your Portfolio and Staying Organized

One of the most overlooked aspects of managing cryptocurrency is keeping your portfolio organized and your records accurate. In the fast-moving world of digital assets, it's easy to lose track of what you own, when you bought it, where it's stored, and how it's performing. Without proper tracking, you risk making poor decisions, missing profit-taking opportunities, or facing major headaches when tax season arrives.

The first step in staying organized is **consolidating your information**. Many investors spread their crypto across multiple exchanges, wallets, and blockchains. This makes it harder to get a clear picture of your total holdings. Start by listing all the platforms where you have assets — centralized exchanges, hot wallets, cold wallets, DeFi platforms, and staking accounts. Include each coin or token, the amount, the date of purchase, and the purchase price.

To make this easier, consider using **crypto portfolio tracking tools** like CoinStats, CoinGecko, Delta, or Blockfolio. These apps allow you to connect your wallets and exchange accounts through secure API keys or by manually entering transactions. With a single dashboard, you can see your total portfolio value, individual asset performance, and historical trends. Many trackers also send alerts for price changes or portfolio milestones, helping you react quickly to market moves.

In addition to portfolio tracking, **transaction record-keeping** is essential. Every buy, sell, swap, transfer, and staking reward should be documented. Not only does this help you stay organized, but it also makes tax reporting much simpler. Many countries require you to report capital gains or income from crypto, and without accurate records, you could end up overpaying or underreporting. Using specialized crypto tax software like Koinly, CoinTracker, or TokenTax can automate much of this process by importing your transaction history and generating reports.

When tracking your portfolio, it's important to note **where your assets are stored**. Always know which wallet or platform holds each coin and the recovery method for that wallet. For cold wallets, keep a secure, offline record of your seed phrases and backup instructions. For hot wallets and exchanges, ensure you have 2FA enabled and up-to-date contact information.

A good tracking system also includes **performance reviews**. At least once a month, evaluate your portfolio's balance. Are you too heavily invested in one coin? Is a particular asset underperforming? Are you holding too much on exchanges instead of in secure storage? Regular reviews help you make informed rebalancing decisions and adjust your strategy to match market conditions and your long-term goals.

Security should always be part of your organization plan. Keep your portfolio records stored securely — not in an unencrypted file on your computer or a public cloud folder. Consider using encrypted drives, password-protected spreadsheets, or even physical notebooks stored in safe locations. Remember that while tracking tools are helpful, they should never require you to share your private keys.

Lastly, organization is not a one-time effort — it's an ongoing habit. The crypto market moves quickly, and your holdings can change just as fast. By consistently updating your records, reviewing performance, and knowing exactly where and how your assets are stored, you not only protect your investment but also set yourself up for more confident decision-making in the future.

Learning to track your holdings

Ethan had never thought much about tracking his portfolio. He checked his crypto balances every few days, but it was always on whichever exchange or wallet app he happened to be using at the moment. His Bitcoin sat on his Ledger, his Cardano was staked in Daedalus, and a few smaller coins lived on Binance. In his mind, it was all "safe," so there wasn't much else to do.

One evening, while scrolling through a crypto forum, he saw a post titled *"I just found $1,200 worth of tokens I forgot I owned."* The story described how someone had bought a small amount of a coin months earlier, forgotten about it, and only rediscovered it while going through old transaction records. Ethan chuckled — until he remembered a $50 purchase of a small altcoin he'd made months ago on a decentralized exchange. He hadn't checked it since.

Curious, he opened his MetaMask wallet and realized the coin wasn't even visible on his default list. He had to manually import the contract address from CoinGecko. When he did, his jaw dropped — the $50 was now worth $480. If he hadn't checked, he might have missed the chance to take profit entirely.

That moment was a wake-up call. He grabbed a notebook and started writing down every coin he owned, where it was stored, when he bought it, and what he paid. The list quickly grew longer than he expected. Between exchanges, hot wallets, cold wallets, and staking accounts, his portfolio was more scattered than he thought.

Lucas suggested he try a portfolio tracker. Ethan downloaded CoinStats and connected it to his Coinbase and Binance accounts using secure API keys. For his Ledger and staking wallets, he entered the transactions manually. Within an hour he had his entire crypto picture on one screen for the first time. Seeing the numbers together made him realize two things: he was overly concentrated in just three coins, and he had too much value sitting on exchanges instead of in cold storage.

He began setting monthly reminders to review his portfolio. On the first weekend of each month, he checked prices, updated his holdings, and made small adjustments — moving excess funds to his Ledger, rebalancing between coins, and noting any staking rewards. He also started downloading CSV transaction histories from each platform and storing them in an encrypted folder on an external hard drive, knowing they'd be crucial for taxes.

Over time, the process became second nature. Whenever he made a new purchase, he added it to his tracker and logged the details in his spreadsheet. He began to see patterns — coins he held too long, investments that performed better than expected, and fees that were eating into his returns.

A few months later, another market rally hit. Thanks to his organized records, Ethan knew exactly which holdings had reached his profit target. Instead of guessing or scrambling to remember purchase prices, he acted confidently, selling portions and moving the gains to stablecoins.

Ethan realized that tracking wasn't just about numbers — it was about control. By staying organized, he no longer felt like he was reacting to the market. Instead, he was running his portfolio like a business, with clear records, a plan, and the ability to make decisions quickly when opportunities appeared.

Chapter 8: Staying Safe with DeFi, NFTs, and Emerging Crypto Trends

As cryptocurrency evolves, new sectors like decentralized finance (DeFi), non-fungible tokens (NFTs), and emerging blockchain innovations offer exciting opportunities — but they also bring new risks. For many investors, these areas represent the "next frontier" of crypto, where returns can be high but volatility, scams, and technical pitfalls are equally intense. If you decide to explore these trends, your first priority should be understanding the landscape and protecting your assets.

Decentralized Finance (DeFi) refers to blockchain-based applications that offer financial services without traditional intermediaries like banks. With DeFi, you can lend, borrow, earn interest, trade assets, or participate in liquidity pools — all through smart contracts on blockchains like Ethereum, Polygon, and Binance Smart Chain. While DeFi can offer higher yields than centralized platforms, it requires extra caution. Smart contracts are immutable once deployed, so a bug or exploit can drain funds instantly. Before using a DeFi protocol, research its security audits, track record, and community reputation. Start small to test the process, and avoid locking away more than you can afford to lose.

Non-Fungible Tokens (NFTs) have expanded beyond digital art into gaming, collectibles, music, and even tokenized real estate. While some NFTs have sold for millions, the market is highly speculative, and many projects lose value quickly. If buying NFTs, verify the creator's identity, check the project's roadmap, and confirm that the artwork or asset is truly unique and stored on a reliable blockchain. Be wary of "right-click save" copies — the value is in the verified ownership recorded on-chain, not just the image itself. Also, watch out for counterfeit collections on popular NFT marketplaces.

Another emerging area is **play-to-earn (P2E) gaming** and metaverse platforms. These often involve purchasing in-game NFTs or tokens that can be traded or sold. While some have strong communities and real earning potential, others collapse quickly when user growth slows. Always assess whether the platform's economics are sustainable, and avoid spending large sums on assets tied to a single game or app.

Security in these emerging sectors requires specialized awareness. In DeFi, **rug pulls** — where developers abandon a project after taking investors' funds — are a common risk. In NFTs, **phishing sites** disguised as legitimate marketplaces can steal wallet access if you connect without checking the URL. Protect yourself by using a dedicated wallet for experimental or high-risk activities, separate from your main holdings. This way, if something goes wrong, your core assets remain safe.

Also understand that emerging trends are magnets for **FOMO-driven hype cycles**. Social media can amplify excitement around a new protocol, NFT drop, or metaverse land sale, pushing prices up temporarily. When hype fades, many participants are left holding devalued assets. The best defense is to approach every new trend with skepticism, take time to research, and resist the urge to "ape in" just because others are doing it.

Finally, document every transaction, just as you would with standard crypto investments. Many DeFi and NFT platforms do not provide simple tax reports, so keeping your own records will save time later. For DeFi activities, note the date, token amount, and platform used. For NFTs, record the purchase price, transaction fees, and sale details if applicable.

Exploring DeFi, NFTs, and new crypto trends can expand your experience and potentially your profits — but only if you treat them with the same discipline, security practices, and long-term thinking as the rest of your portfolio. In these fast-changing spaces, caution is not a weakness — it's your greatest asset.

How Ethan learned to stay safe

Ethan had heard about DeFi for months, but it always sounded like a world reserved for crypto veterans. That changed when Lucas messaged him late one night: "You've got to check this new staking platform — people are making 15% APY." The number made Ethan's eyebrows rise. Fifteen percent was more than any bank would offer in a decade.

Curiosity won out. He visited the site, which was sleek and polished, with animated charts and glowing testimonials. Before diving in, he remembered his new rule — research first, invest later. He searched for reviews, read the project's whitepaper, and looked up whether it had been audited by a security firm. To his relief, it had two public audits and a small but active community on Discord. Still, he decided to start with a small deposit of stablecoins.

The process was a bit intimidating — connecting his wallet, approving the smart contract, and watching the confirmation appear on the blockchain explorer. Over the next few days, he saw his balance slowly grow. But then he noticed something on the forum: another user posted a warning about a "rug pull" on a similar-looking project with almost the same name. The only difference was a single letter in the web address. Ethan double-checked that he was on the correct site and bookmarked it immediately, realizing how easy it would be to fall into a lookalike scam.

Not long after, Ethan's interest shifted to NFTs. He'd seen celebrities posting about million-dollar digital art sales, but he wasn't looking to spend that kind of money. Instead, he wanted something affordable and meaningful. Browsing a popular NFT marketplace, he found a collection of digital photographs from a travel photographer whose work he admired. The price was reasonable, and owning a unique blockchain-verified piece of art appealed to him.

Before clicking "buy," Ethan checked the creator's profile to make sure it wasn't a copycat account. He verified the social media links, saw that the artist had an active following, and confirmed that the NFTs were minted from the official wallet. Feeling confident, he purchased his first NFT. When it appeared in his wallet, it wasn't just a picture — it was a small personal victory in understanding how digital ownership worked.

A few weeks later, a friend invited him into a "private" group chat about a new play-to-earn game. "It's early access," the friend claimed, "and the in-game NFTs could triple in value." The screenshots looked impressive, but Ethan noticed the developers were anonymous and the website had no audit history. Remembering the rug pull warning, he passed on the opportunity. Two months later, news spread that the game's creators had vanished, taking millions in player funds with them.

Through these experiences, Ethan learned that the excitement of DeFi, NFTs, and other emerging crypto trends could be both thrilling and dangerous. By starting small, verifying everything, and keeping his high-value holdings separate from his "experimental" wallet, he was able to explore without risking his financial foundation.

For Ethan, the takeaway was clear: innovation in crypto moved fast, but caution had to move faster.

Chapter 9: Building a Long-Term Crypto Strategy

A successful crypto journey isn't just about buying the right coins or avoiding scams — it's about having a long-term plan that guides your decisions no matter what the market is doing. Without a strategy, it's easy to fall into emotional investing, chasing quick gains during bull markets and panic-selling during downturns. A clear plan keeps you disciplined, helps you manage risk, and aligns your investments with your personal financial goals.

The first step in building a long-term crypto strategy is defining **your purpose**. Ask yourself why you are investing in crypto in the first place. Is it to build wealth for retirement, to diversify your investment portfolio, to support blockchain innovation, or to speculate for higher short-term gains? Your reason will shape your time horizon, risk tolerance, and portfolio composition.

Once you've defined your purpose, you need to set a **time horizon**. Long-term strategies typically span years, not weeks or months. If your goal is retirement savings in 20 years, your approach will be very different from someone aiming to buy a house in three years. Longer time frames allow for more aggressive allocations since you have time to recover from volatility. Shorter time frames require more conservative asset choices to preserve capital.

Next, decide on your **asset allocation**. A balanced crypto portfolio might include a mix of blue-chip cryptocurrencies like Bitcoin and Ethereum, mid-cap projects with strong fundamentals, and a small percentage of higher-risk, high-reward coins or emerging sectors like DeFi or NFTs. Many investors adopt the "core and satellite" approach — the majority of the portfolio is in stable, proven assets, while a smaller portion is allocated to more speculative opportunities.

Risk management is critical to any long-term plan. One of the most effective tools is **position sizing** — determining how much of your total portfolio you are willing to risk on a single asset or trade. This prevents a single bad investment from wiping out your gains. Another key principle is diversification, not just across coins, but across storage methods, platforms, and even blockchains. This reduces the impact of any one failure, such as an exchange hack or a project collapse.

You also need a clear **buying and selling strategy**. For many long-term investors, **dollar-cost averaging (DCA)** is a powerful method — investing a fixed amount at regular intervals, regardless of price. This reduces the emotional impact of market swings and ensures consistent accumulation.

For selling, set profit-taking levels in advance, such as selling a portion of your holdings when an asset doubles or triples in value, while leaving the rest to ride future gains.

A long-term strategy should also include **contingency planning**. Crypto markets are unpredictable, and sudden events like regulatory changes, exchange failures, or network hacks can impact your holdings. Consider creating an "emergency exit" plan that outlines what you will do if a major negative event occurs.

Finally, commit to **continuous learning**. The blockchain space evolves rapidly, with new technologies, regulations, and opportunities emerging constantly. Make it a habit to read market updates, follow credible analysts, and review your portfolio regularly. This ensures that your strategy remains relevant and adaptable.

The ultimate goal of a long-term crypto strategy is to remove guesswork and reduce stress. When you know your objectives, your risk limits, and your process for buying and selling, you can ride out market volatility with confidence — turning crypto from a gamble into a disciplined, purpose-driven investment.

The story of how Ethan learned to build a long-term crypto strategy

Ethan had been in the crypto world for over a year now. He'd made mistakes, learned from them, and even pulled in some small profits. But his approach was still reactive — buying coins when they caught his attention, selling when he felt nervous, and jumping on opportunities because someone in a group chat sounded convincing. He knew this wasn't sustainable.

One Sunday morning, Ethan sat at his kitchen table with a cup of coffee and a notepad. He decided it was time to treat his crypto like a serious investment, not a hobby. The first question he wrote down was simple: *Why am I doing this?* At first, he thought the answer was "to make money," but the more he thought about it, the more specific he became. He wanted to build wealth over the next decade, not just flip coins for quick wins. That meant adopting a long-term mindset.

He set his time horizon at ten years. That gave him space to ride out bear markets and focus on projects with staying power. He wrote down that at least 70% of his portfolio would be in proven assets like Bitcoin and Ethereum, with 20% in strong mid-cap coins, and only 10% reserved for high-risk, high-reward plays like emerging DeFi tokens or metaverse projects.

For the first time, Ethan set rules for buying and selling. He decided to use dollar-cost averaging to steadily add to his positions, buying a fixed amount every two weeks no matter the market price. For selling, he set clear targets: when an asset doubled, he'd take back his original investment and let the rest ride. If an asset tripled or quadrupled, he'd skim more profits but keep a core position intact.

He also developed an emergency plan. If a major regulatory change or exchange failure threatened his holdings, he would move assets to cold storage immediately and pause all new investments until the dust settled. Knowing he had a plan for bad scenarios gave him a sense of calm.

Ethan's new strategy changed how he felt during market swings. When Bitcoin dipped 15% in a week, he didn't panic — he just stuck to his DCA schedule and bought more. When a speculative altcoin he'd bought with "fun money" crashed by 70%, he wasn't shaken, because it was only a tiny portion of his portfolio.

Six months later, his portfolio hadn't just grown — it felt more stable, more intentional. The constant stress and second-guessing were gone. He didn't feel the need to check prices every hour. He knew his goals, his allocations, and his rules, and that gave him confidence no bull or bear market could take away.

For Ethan, building a long-term crypto strategy wasn't just about making better investments — it was about taking control. It turned chaos into clarity and made the unpredictable world of crypto feel, for the first time, like something he could master.

Chapter 10: Keeping Up With Crypto and Adapting Your Plan

The cryptocurrency space moves at an extraordinary pace. New projects launch daily, regulations shift unexpectedly, technologies evolve, and market cycles turn faster than most traditional asset classes. If you want to succeed long term, you can't simply set a strategy and forget it — you need to stay informed, monitor changes, and adapt when necessary, all while maintaining discipline and avoiding reactionary moves.

The first element of staying current is **information gathering**. Choose a handful of reliable news sources and industry analysts to follow regularly. Websites like CoinDesk, The Block, and CoinTelegraph provide daily updates, while blockchain-specific explorers and analytics tools give you on-chain insights into what's happening in real time. Be selective — following too many sources can lead to information overload and conflicting advice.

Social media can be both a valuable and dangerous tool. Platforms like Twitter (X) and Reddit often break news before mainstream outlets, but they're also rife with rumors, hype, and misinformation. Learn to identify credible voices: look for people who provide data, show their reasoning, and have a track record of accuracy. Avoid acting on information that can't be verified from multiple independent sources.

Another key is **understanding market cycles**. Crypto tends to move in cycles driven by sentiment, adoption, and macroeconomic conditions. Bull markets can create a false sense of security, while bear markets can test your conviction. By studying past cycles and tracking metrics like trading volume, funding rates, and the Bitcoin halving schedule, you can better anticipate broad trends — without trying to time the market perfectly.

Your **long-term plan** should be flexible enough to adapt to new information without losing its core structure. For example, if a major regulatory change impacts one of your holdings, you may need to reallocate funds or adjust your profit targets. If a new technology or sector emerges, you might dedicate a small portion of your portfolio to exploring it. Adaptation is about making calculated changes, not chasing every new trend.

Ongoing education is crucial. Take time to learn about emerging areas like layer-2 scaling solutions, cross-chain interoperability, decentralized identity, and other innovations. Even if you choose not to invest directly in these areas, understanding them helps you see where the industry is heading. Online courses, webinars, podcasts, and developer blogs are excellent learning tools.

Regular **portfolio reviews** are part of staying updated. At least quarterly, assess your holdings against your goals, risk tolerance, and the current market environment. Has the fundamental thesis for each asset changed? Are your allocations still balanced? Is there an asset that has grown disproportionately large due to price appreciation and now needs trimming to reduce risk?

Finally, balance your engagement with the market. It's easy to burn out if you're constantly monitoring prices and news. Set a schedule for checking your portfolio and stick to it. Trust the strategy you've built, and remember that in crypto, patience is as important as speed.

Staying informed and adaptable doesn't mean abandoning discipline — it means making sure your strategy remains relevant as the crypto landscape evolves. By combining continuous learning with thoughtful adjustments, you can navigate the rapid pace of change and position yourself for sustained success.

Learning to adapt your plan

Ethan had finally reached a point where he felt confident in his long-term crypto strategy. His portfolio was balanced, his goals were clear, and he had systems in place for buying, storing, and tracking his assets. But he knew the crypto world didn't stand still. Projects that seemed unstoppable could fade, and new opportunities could appear overnight. If he wanted to stay ahead, he needed a way to keep informed without drowning in noise.

He began by curating his information sources. At first, he'd followed dozens of Twitter accounts, joined every Telegram group he could find, and subscribed to every crypto newsletter that popped up in his feed. But it was overwhelming — too many conflicting opinions, too much hype. So he trimmed it down to a handful of trusted voices: a blockchain developer who explained technical updates in plain English, a market analyst who focused on long-term trends, and a few industry news sites that reported facts before rumors.

Every morning, Ethan spent 20 minutes scanning headlines and checking updates from these sources. If something caught his attention — a new regulation, a major network upgrade, or a security incident — he'd dig deeper before deciding whether it affected his holdings. This process helped him filter out the noise and avoid making impulsive decisions based on incomplete information.

One afternoon, he read that one of the mid-cap coins in his portfolio was undergoing a major protocol change. The upgrade promised faster transactions and lower fees, but it also required users to migrate their tokens to a new chain. Ethan knew that if he missed the migration deadline, his old tokens could become worthless. Because he had a habit of checking reliable news daily, he caught the update in time, followed the official instructions, and avoided losing a significant part of his investment.

He also learned to review his portfolio quarterly. Every three months, he would look at each asset and ask: *Has the original reason I bought this still valid? Has the project delivered on its roadmap? Has the risk profile changed?* Sometimes the answer was yes, and he would hold or even increase his position. Other times, he realized it was time to take profits or cut losses and reallocate into stronger projects.

Ethan avoided chasing every new trend, but he remained open to exploring them cautiously. When NFTs first exploded in popularity, he didn't jump in immediately. Instead, he spent a few weeks learning about the technology, the marketplaces, and the risks. Only when he understood the basics did he buy his first one — a modest purchase he could afford to lose. This approach kept him curious but disciplined.

Over time, Ethan noticed a change in his mindset. He no longer felt anxious when the market dipped or euphoric when it spiked. He had confidence that his strategy could adapt without being thrown off course. And most importantly, he had a clear process for staying informed, filtering out hype, and acting deliberately.

For Ethan, the crypto journey was no longer a wild ride he was trying to survive — it was a long-term voyage he was navigating with a steady hand and a clear map.

Epilogue: The Journey Ahead

When Ethan first dipped his toes into the crypto world, it was with cautious curiosity and a sense of uncertainty. What started as a simple Bitcoin purchase quickly evolved into a deeper understanding of security, storage, scams, transactions, staking, and long-term strategy. Along the way, he learned that success in cryptocurrency wasn't about luck or chasing hype — it was about knowledge, preparation, and discipline.

This journey mirrors the experience of many who venture into digital assets. At the beginning, everything feels new, complex, and risky. The temptation is to rush — to buy quickly, to act on tips, to join whatever is trending. But as Ethan's story shows, slowing down, asking the right questions, and building a foundation of safe practices transforms the experience from speculative gambling into strategic investing.

Throughout this book, we've explored the practical steps to buy, store, and use crypto securely. We've seen how to choose exchanges wisely, protect private keys, spot and avoid scams, make transactions with precision, and put crypto to work through payments and passive income. We've looked at how to exit safely back into cash, keep a portfolio organized, explore new sectors like DeFi and NFTs without recklessness, build a strategy for the long term, and adapt as the market evolves.

Ethan's progression from a hesitant beginner to a confident investor reflects the real reward of learning — not just financial gains, but peace of mind. The anxiety that once came with market swings has been replaced by clarity, the fear of losing everything by mistake replaced by protective systems and habits. He now treats his crypto like any other serious investment: with respect, patience, and an eye toward the future.

For you, the reader, the path forward will be uniquely your own. You may choose to focus on a few core assets, or explore emerging technologies with a small allocation. You may prioritize passive income through staking, or see crypto as part of a broader portfolio. The specific choices matter less than the principles guiding them: security first, research always, and a willingness to adapt without abandoning your plan.

The crypto space will continue to change — faster than most industries. There will be new coins, new scams, new regulations, and new opportunities. But armed with the lessons from this journey, you can navigate these changes with confidence. You'll know when to explore and when to step back, when to act decisively and when to wait.

In the end, cryptocurrency is about more than digital money. It's about control — control over your assets, your decisions, and your future. The tools, technologies, and markets will evolve, but the core truth will remain: your greatest asset in crypto is not the coins you hold, but the knowledge and habits that protect them.

As you continue your own crypto journey, take these lessons with you. Use them to make better decisions, avoid costly mistakes, and seize opportunities wisely. Whether the road ahead leads to new heights or tests your patience, you'll walk it with the confidence that comes from knowing you've built your foundation the right way.

www.ingramcontent.com/pod-product-compliance
Ingram Content Group UK Ltd.
Pitfield, Milton Keynes, MK11 3LW, UK
UKHW020156290926
15471UKWH00005B/895

9 798349 640902